D0787094

religion in focus
buddhism

Geoff Teece

First published in 2003 by Franklin Watts
Franklin Watts, 96 Leonard Street, London EC2A 4XD

Franklin Watts Australia
45–51 Huntley Street, Alexandria, NSW 2015
This edition published under license from Franklin Watts. All rights reserved.

Copyright © 2003 Franklin Watts

Series Editor: Adrian Cole; Designer: Proof Books; Art Director: Jonathan Hair; Consultant: Clive
Erricker, Inspector for Religious Education (Hampshire); Picture Researcher: Diana Morris

Published in the United States by Smart Apple Media
1980 Lookout Drive, North Mankato, Minnesota 56003

Library of Congress Cataloging-in-Publication Data

Teece, Geoff.
Buddhism / Geoff Teece.
p. cm. — (Religion in focus)
Includes index.
Summary: Discusses the beliefs and practices of Buddhism, which has some 328 million adherents
worldwide.
ISBN 1-58340-464-3
1. Buddhism—Juvenile literature. [1. Buddhism.] I. Title. II. Series.

BQ4032.T33 2004
294.3—dc22   2003190055

9 8 7 6 5 4 3 2 1

Acknowledgments
The publishers would like to thank the following for permission to reproduce photographs
in this book:

T. Bognar/Trip: 9t. British Library, London/Bridgeman Art Library: 13t.
David Cumming/Eye Ubiquitous: 20c, 23c. Bennett Dean/Eye Ubiquitous: 5b.
B. Gadsby/Trip: 7. A. Gasson/Trip: 1, 18. F. Good/Trip: 21t. John Hulme/Eye
Ubiquitous: 10, 15b, 26. R. Nichols/Trip:5t. Christine Osborne/World Religions PL:
15t, 21b, 23t, 28t. Tim Page/Eye Ubiquitous: 28b. C. Rennie/Trip: 20t.
H. Rogers/Trip: 3, 8, 27t, 27c. Paul Seheult/Eye Ubiquitous: 6c. Paul Thompson/Eye
Ubiquitous: 23b. P. Treanor/Trip: 22. Trip: 9b, 30t. Bob Turner/Trip: 13b. B. Vikander/
Trip: 19. Julia Waterlow/Eye Ubiquitous: 16. John Wender/Eye Ubiquitous: 6t.

SPELLINGS USED IN THIS BOOK

Many Buddhist words can be spelled in two ways. The Theravada
scriptures were originally written in Pali and the Mahayana
scriptures were written in Sanskrit. For example, *nibbana* in Pali is
nirvana in Sanskrit, *sutta* in Pali is *sutra* in Sanskrit, and the *Dhamma*
in Pali is *Dharma* in Sanskrit. To avoid confusion, Pali spellings are
used throughout this book.

Contents

Origins and history

Buddhism is one of the great world religions. It began in India and is now the main religion in such countries as Sri Lanka, Bhutan, Myanmar, Thailand, Cambodia, and Vietnam. Today, Buddhists are also found in many parts of Europe, the Americas, Australia, and Asia.

One of the things that distinguishes Buddhism from other religions is that Buddhists do not believe in God. Instead, they follow the teachings of a historical figure known as the Buddha. The Buddha is not a name, but a title which means "enlightened one." The goal of all Buddhists is to become enlightened like the Buddha.

The Buddha did not actually teach that there was no God. He just did not want people to be distracted by worrying about whether or not God existed. He taught that people are attached to their desires. This causes suffering both to them and to others. But if people free themselves from their desires, they can attain *nibbana*, a state of perfect bliss in which people see things as they really are. The Buddha taught people to achieve *nibbana* by their own efforts, or "skillful means" (*upaya*).

BUDDHIST POPULATION

It is estimated that there are more than 328 million Buddhists in the world.

Buddhist majority
large communities
small communities
scattering of Buddhists

1 India
2 Sri Lanka
3 Bhutan
4 Myanmar
5 Thailand
6 Cambodia
7 Vietnam
8 Nepal
9 China
10 Japan

BUDDHISM SPREADS

The Buddha lived in an area of northeast India that is now Nepal, in the fifth century B.C. He lived for about 80 years. After his death, Buddhism spread all around India, and by the third century B.C., its teachings had reached such places as Sri Lanka and Burma (now called Myanmar). The religion spread to China in the first century A.D. and to Japan by the sixth century A.D. By A.D. 624, Tibet had also discovered Buddhism.

FORMS OF BUDDHISM

As Buddhism spread, it adopted aspects of each new country's culture, so Buddhism in one country can seem very different from Buddhism in another. However, while the practices may be different, the basic teachings, called *Dhamma*, remain the same.

THERAVADA BUDDHISM

Theravada (way of the elders) is the oldest form of Buddhism. It is sometimes known as southern Buddhism because it is found mainly in Sri Lanka and southeast Asia. Theravada Buddhists believe that they follow a path that is closest to the words of the Buddha, and they regard a monk's or nun's way of living (*vinaya*) as the best way to become enlightened. Theravada Buddhist monks wear saffron yellow robes.

THERAVADA MONKS
A group of young monks in saffron robes. Many boys become monks for a short time as part of their spiritual education.

MAHAYANA BUDDHISM

As well as spreading south from India, Buddhism moved north and east to places such as Tibet, Nepal, China, and Japan. In these countries, people follow a form of Buddhism called *Mahayana* (the great way, or career). This focuses on compassion—a very deep caring for other people. Such compassion is shown in the form of a *bodhisattva*, an enlightened person who has put off reaching *nibbana* in order to help other people towards enlightenment. There are several different schools within Mahayana Buddhism, including Tibetan, Zen, and Pure Land Buddhism. Tibetan Buddhist monks and nuns wear maroon-colored robes. Their leader is the Dalai Lama, who now lives in exile in northern India.

VAJRAYANA BUDDHISM

Another form of Buddhism, called *Vajrayana* (the Diamond Way), spread from India to Tibet, Bhutan, and Mongolia around A.D. 700. Some call this Tantric Buddhism, because it was influenced by an ancient Indian tradition called Tantra.

MAHAYANA MONKS
Mahayana monks wear maroon-colored robes.

FRIENDS OF THE WESTERN BUDDHIST ORDER

Most forms of Buddhism can be found in the West, and in 1967, a western Buddhist movement called the Friends of the Western Buddhist Order was founded. This includes aspects of many of the different schools mentioned above. Its main goal is to allow people to practice Buddhism in a way that is suited to their western way of living.

Siddhattha Gotama (The Buddha)

SITTING BUDDHA
A typical statue of the Buddha sitting in the lotus position. This is how he sat when he reached enlightenment.

The Buddha was not a god, or even a prophet, but a human being named Siddhattha Gotama. Buddhists believe that what he taught—the *Dhamma*—is eternal, and that there were many other Buddhas before him. But Buddhism as we know it today began with Siddhattha. His life story is important because it shows how a young man grappled with the truth of "how things really are."

THE BUDDHA'S BIRTH AND EARLY LIFE

Siddhattha's father was the chief of the Sakya people, who came from a place now called Nepal. As members of the ruling class, his family lived in a palace, and Siddhattha had a rich and privileged upbringing. His background was influenced by the Hindu religion, and much of what the Buddha taught stemmed from Hindu ideas.

Before Siddhattha was born, his mother had a dream about a white elephant. This was considered a sign that her son would grow up to be someone very special. At the boy's birth, a wise man told Siddhattha's father that if his son was kept away from the sorrows and reality of life, he would grow up to be a powerful king. If, on the other hand, Siddhattha did learn about or see the sorrows and reality of life, he would grow up and leave home to be a great teacher. His father wanted his son to be happy and so decided to keep him sheltered from the world. Siddhattha had everything he could want, including a beautiful wife and son, but his father did not allow him to leave the palace grounds. This made him restless and unhappy.

BUDDHA'S BIRTH
Many Buddhist temples contain paintings depicting scenes from the Buddha's life.

THE FOUR SIGHTS

One day, Siddhattha persuaded Chanda, his charioteer, to take him for a drive outside the palace. He saw four sights:

1. An old wrinkled man.
2. A sick person in great pain.
3. A dead person.
4. A contented-looking monk wearing saffron robes.

LOOKING FOR ANSWERS

Back in the palace, Siddhattha began to realize that all people grow old, get sick, and die. He thought constantly about the problems and causes of suffering. At the age of 29, Siddhattha and Chanda left the palace for good. Siddhattha cut off his hair and put on simple clothes. He searched for someone who could answer the questions that had been troubling him. Remembering the contented-looking monk, Siddhattha visited religious teachers. They told him to give up everything he owned and live as an ascetic (someone who practices self-denial and rejects worldly comforts).

So, accompanied by five friends, Siddhattha took on this way of life. He fasted (went without food) for long periods. Eventually, when he was nearly starving, Siddhattha decided that this way was not helping him. His friends left him, upset that he was giving up. But Siddhattha had learned that neither great riches nor extreme poverty and hunger could make him happy or answer his questions. There must be a middle way between these two paths.

ENLIGHTENMENT

Siddhattha sat under a tree in Bodh Gaya, in northern India, and meditated for 49 days and 49 nights in the hope of finding the truth. He went into deep meditation until he reached a state of complete wisdom and understanding known as "enlightenment." The tree under which Siddhattha sat is known as the Bodhi (enlightenment) tree. It was from this time that Siddhattha became known as the Buddha.

After his enlightenment, the Buddha walked from Gaya to Sarnath near Varanasi in India, where he found his five friends in the deer park. Here he preached his first sermon, and his friends became his followers, as did his family. For 35 years, he taught what he had discovered through enlightenment to crowds all over northeast India.

THE BUDDHA'S DEATH

When the Buddha reached the age of 80, he knew he was ready to die. He called his followers to him and asked if they had any questions about his teaching. His last words were, "All things change. Keep up your effort." The Buddha's death is called *parinibbana* (the final passing into *nibbana*).

RECLINING BUDDHA
When the Buddha died he lay on his side. This image of the Buddha represents his *parinibbana*.

Enlightenment

The goal of all Buddhists is to reach *nibbana*, which literally means "snuffing out." This is a snuffing out of what Buddhists call the three fires, or three poisons—ignorance, hatred, and greed. When the Buddha became enlightened, he realized that these poisons are the cause of all human suffering. In order to reach *nibbana*, people have to be free of them. Buddhists believe that this can take many lifetimes to achieve.

THE THREE POISONS:
1. Ignorance
2. Hatred
3. Greed

THE BUDDHA SITTING ON A LOTUS FLOWER

This picture is one of many that show the Buddha sitting on a lotus flower while meditating under the Bodhi tree. This is where he reached enlightenment.

REBIRTH AND KAMMA

Buddhists believe that when a person dies, he or she is born again (reborn) as another human being or an animal, perhaps in a different place. The reborn form depends on a person's *kamma* (action).

According to the law of kamma, if a person lives a good life, good things will lead to a better life next time. To count as "good," a person has to develop "merit." This means doing worthy deeds such as practicing devotion, or worship, and serving the monks (*dana*). A person must also develop compassion (*karuna*) and loving kindness (*metta*)—caring for all living things. Many Buddhists meditate to wish all living things happiness.

WHO CAN REACH ENLIGHTENMENT?

Buddhists believe that all people can become enlightened. It is said that when the Buddha was sitting under the Bodhi tree, he looked out over a pool filled with lotus plants. Some plants had unopened buds on them, while others had flowers that were fully opened. The Buddha compared the flowers to people in various stages of enlightenment. The fully opened lotus is like a person who is ready to take in the *Dhamma*. Because of this, the lotus has become a symbol of enlightenment for Buddhists.

REACHING NIBBANA

When someone reaches *nibbana* they are in a state of perfect happiness, free from the three poisons (*see opposite*). It might seem that a person can only reach *nibbana* when they die. But this is not the case. *Nibbana* is simply a state of being where there is no suffering left inside and no longer any need to be reborn.

Different schools of Buddhism believe different things about how *nibbana* is reached. Theravada Buddhists say that a person should try to become an *arahat* (enlightened saint). This is someone who has let go of attachment to the three poisons through personal effort. They believe that this is what the Buddha originally taught. Mahayana Buddhists say that people should try to become *bodhisattvas*—enlightened ones who have delayed entering *nibbana* because they have great compassion and want to help other people reach *nibbana*. Some *bodhisattvas* return to this world, and some live in a kind of heavenly land, often called the "Pure Land."

ACHIEVING PARINIBBANA

When an enlightened person dies, they enter *parinibbana* (final *nibbana*). Some Buddhists describe this as reaching a "pure land" that is free from pain.

THE LOTUS FLOWER
The flower of the lotus plant symbolizes enlightenment in Indian religions.

BODHISATTVA
A Mahayana Buddhist aims to become a *bodhisattva*, an enlightened being full of compassion.

The Sangha

THE THREE JEWELS OR
REFUGES OF BUDDHISM:
1. the Buddha
2. the *Dhamma*
3. the *Sangha*

Traditional Buddhist teaching says that a Buddha appears only once every 320,000 years. Siddhattha Gotama is the Buddha of this age, so his teachings—the *Dhamma*—have to be kept alive. This is the job of the *Sangha* (assembly) which is the name for the Buddhist community. When a person becomes a Buddhist, he or she makes a commitment to the Three Jewels—or Three Refuges—by reciting these vows: "I take refuge in the Buddha, I take refuge in the *Dhamma*, I take refuge in the *Sangha*."

THE TWO GROUPS OF THE SANGHA

The *Sangha* is made up of two groups: the monks and nuns, who are ordained (trained and appointed), and the "lay" members, who are not. In Japan, there are ordained priests as well as monks. Buddhist monks and nuns are celibate (they do not marry), but priests, who look after the temples, may marry.

The two groups of the *Sangha* were established at the time of the Buddha, when some of his early followers decided to give up their family lives to renounce the world and spread the *Dhamma*. These first monks were called *bhikkhus* and the nuns *bhikkunis*. They followed the

THE TWO GROUPS MEET
Food from a lay Buddhist is collected in an alms bowl by two young monks.

10

Buddha's example, shaved their heads, and wore saffron yellow robes. Not all of the Buddha's followers became monks or nuns. Others stayed with their families, but practiced the Buddha's teachings. They became the lay members of the *Sangha*, supporting the *bhikkhus* and *bhikkunis* with food that they collected in alms bowls.

ORDAINED AND LAY BUDDHISTS

Today, the balance between ordained and lay members of the *Sangha* varies between different Buddhist groups. The Friends of the Western Buddhist Order believe anyone in their community can be ordained; male or female, single or married. Ordination in this tradition does not mean becoming a monk or a nun. Some ordained members choose to live at home with their families, while others join other Buddhists in separate communities. For Western Buddhists, being ordained means making a public promise to live by Buddhist values.

For most Buddhists, however, ordination means becoming a monk or a nun. Monks and nuns are not allowed to earn money and traditionally they have very few possessions. They follow the lifestyle of the Buddha by separating themselves from material things and worldly concerns. All Buddhists promise to follow a set of guidelines called the Five Precepts (*see right and also page 14*), but monks and nuns have 227 rules to live by! As in the early days of Buddhism, the lay members of the community cater to the monks' and nuns' basic needs. This enables lay Buddhists to practice generosity (*dana*). And they in turn can go to the monks and nuns for wisdom and advice.

THE FIVE PRECEPTS:
1. Be kind and avoid harming living things.
2. Be generous and avoid taking things that have not been given.
3. Be content and avoid wrong-doing.
4. Be honest and avoid telling lies.
5. Be clear-minded and avoid drugs and alcohol.

THE EIGHT REQUISITES

Monks and nuns are allowed to own only eight things, called the Eight Requisites. These were set by the Buddha himself. They are:

1. Robes
2. An alms bowl for food
3. A belt
4. A razor for shaving
5. A needle and ball of thread
6. A water filter
7. A walking stick
8. A toothpick

Buddhist scriptures

When the teachings of a religion are written down, they are known as scriptures. There are many Buddhist scriptures, and they all play a part in preserving what the Buddha taught.

PALM-LEAF BOOK
The first copies of the Pali Canon were written on palm leaves.

THERAVADA SCRIPTURES

The Buddha's teachings were traditionally memorized by members of the *Sangha* and passed on by word of mouth. But sometime after his death, the Theravada *Sangha* decided to write them down. They wrote mostly in the Pali language, which was spoken in Sri Lanka in about 80 B.C., and the writings became known as the Pali Canon, or *Tripitaka*.

The Pali Canon is the earliest and most complete collection of Buddhist scriptures. It is sometimes known as the "three baskets" because the first copies were written on palm leaves and kept in baskets.

THE THREE BASKETS

1. The Vinaya Pitaka (basket of discipline).
This contains the rules that the Buddha taught monks and nuns for them to live by.

2. The Sutta Pitaka (basket of discourses).
This makes up over half of the Pali Canon and contains writings called the *Dhammapada* and the *Jataka* Tales. The *Dhammapada* (path or way of *Dhamma*) is a collection of the Buddha's sayings, arranged as 423 verses and split into 26 chapters. Young novice monks have to learn the sayings when they join the *Sangha*. Lay Buddhists also get most of their teachings and inspiration from the *Dhammapada*.

Buddhists believe that in order to become enlightened, a person has to live many lives. Buddha's past lives are laid out in the *Jataka* Tales, which consist of some 500 stories. *Jataka* means "birth story." Many of the tales are about animals because the Buddha was often born into the animal kingdom.

3. The Abhidamma Pitaka (basket of higher teachings).
These writings explore and sum up the teachings of Buddhism.

MAHAYANA SCRIPTURES

When Buddhism spread north to places such as Tibet, more scriptures were created. Many were written in Sanskrit, an ancient Indian language, and later translated into Chinese and Tibetan. These Mahayana scriptures include the *Vinaya Pitaka* and *Sutta Pitaka*, and many others that are not always historically traced back to the Buddha, but which are considered to be higher teachings he did not reveal during his lifetime.

THE LOTUS SUTTA

The best known of the other scriptures is the Lotus *Sutta*, which is especially popular in China and Japan. It explains some of the central ideas of Mahayana Buddhism. This includes the belief that the Buddha, while still focusing on the goal of enlightenment, only taught people what they were capable of understanding. This is often called the "doctrine of skillful means."

HEART AND DIAMOND SUTTAS

Also important to the Mahayana Buddhists are the Heart and Diamond *Suttas*, which teach readers how to become wise. A copy of the Diamond *Sutta* printed in China in A.D. 868 is believed to be the world's oldest existing printed book.

LANGUAGE

The Theravada scriptures were written in Pali, and the Mahayana scriptures were originally in Sanskrit. As a result many Buddhist words can be spelled in two ways. For example, *nibbana* in Pali is *nirvana* in Sanskrit, and *sutta* in Pali is *sutra* in Sanskrit.

A Buddhist guide for living

The roots of Buddhist ethics lie in another set of teachings—the Five Precepts. These underpin all of Buddhist life.

THE FIVE PRECEPTS
The Five Precepts are a guide for living with a positive state of mind. Each precept has two aspects—behavior to avoid, and behavior to develop, or cultivate. The Five Precepts are:

1. Avoid harming any living thing, and cultivate deeds of *metta* (loving kindness).
2. Avoid taking things that you have not been given, and cultivate a generous nature.
3. Avoid sexual wrongdoings, and cultivate simple contentment.
4. Avoid telling lies or speaking unkindly, and cultivate honesty.
5. Avoid drugs and alcohol, and cultivate a pure and clear mind.

All Buddhists try to follow these precepts and chant them regularly. But the Five Precepts are not commandments—they are not forced on people like laws. Buddhists choose to take them on because they want to become like the Buddha.

RULES FOR MONASTIC LIFE
In addition to the Five Precepts, Buddhist monks and nuns follow the *vinaya*. These are rules for monastic life. For novice monks and nuns they include five other precepts:

1. Eating only one meal a day, before noon.
2. Not wearing perfume or jewelry.
3. Going without entertainment.
4. Not possessing money.
5. Not sleeping in a luxurious bed.

For experienced monks and nuns there are 227 precepts in total!

EATING MEAT

Many Buddhists are vegetarian, but this is not a rule all Buddhists have to live by. Some Tibetan Buddhists eat meat, and if a Theravada monk or nun is offered meat as *dana*, they will accept it if the animal has not been killed specifically for them. The emphasis for Buddhists is not to kill on purpose. So, for example, a strict Buddhist could not become a butcher or a fisherman.

A BUDDHIST FAMILY MEAL
This family is eating lunch in a Buddhist temple.

THE LAW OF KAMMA

The Five Precepts are more than just a list of what is right and wrong. Living by them is essential if a Buddhist wants to progress towards enlightenment. This is because another aspect of the Buddha's teaching is the law of *kamma*, which states that everything changes as a result of intentional actions that have outcomes, or consequences. If a Buddhist does things that the Five Precepts teach against, the actions will lead to unhappiness and suffering—not only for them, but also for the world around them.

This law of *kamma* continues after death. If a person stays attached to negative things in life, he or she will be reborn over and over again into *samsara* —a world of birth, sickness, old age, and death. Buddhists believe that by following the Five Precepts and the Noble Eightfold Path (*see pages 18–19*), people can escape this vicious circle of rebirth and suffering.

NOVICE MONKS
These novice monks are being ordained in a mass ceremony in Thailand.

The Dhamma: the Four Noble Truths

The Four Noble Truths form the basis of Buddhist teaching. They help explain what the Buddha realized about life after meditating under the Bodhi tree. His first sermon after enlightenment took place in the deer park at Sarnath. It has become known as the Sermon of the Four Noble Truths, or the Turning of the Wheel of the Law.

THE WHEEL OF LIFE
This is a Tibetan Buddhist symbol, which represents everything Buddhists believe about life and rebirth.

IMPERMANENCE, SUFFERING, AND DESIRE

In the Buddha's sermon he taught the following:

ANNICA (IMPERMANENCE)

Everything in life changes, nothing stays the same. Buddhists call this impermanence *annica*. Because people do not want some things to change—often the good things—people suffer.

DUKKHA (UNSATISFACTORINESS OR SUFFERING)

The suffering caused by *annica* is known as *dukkha*. Suffering is usually associated with negative feelings, such as pain caused by tragedy or illness. However, happy events also cause *dukkha* because they do not last. For example, even the most enjoyable birthday party must eventually come to an end.

TANHA (DESIRE OR CRAVING)

Tanha is the reason that some events cause *dukkha* (suffering). People want good things and they want them to last. For example, a person may not have money to buy the new sneakers they want, so they suffer. They may not want to get old, so they suffer.

However, *annica* can be a positive thing as well as a negative one, because everything changes. This means that bad things such as war, pain, and sadness all come to an end, too. One way of thinking about the Four Noble Truths is to compare them to a curable human disease or illness.

THE FOUR NOBLE TRUTHS

- The first truth is the illness itself—*dukkha*.
  The symptoms are pain, unhappiness, and an unsatisfactory life.

- The second truth is the reason for the illness—*anha*.
  People suffer because they crave things that they cannot have or that do not last.

- The third truth is the prognosis, or outlook for the sufferer.
  The good news is that the illness can be cured.

- The fourth truth is the remedy, or cure for the illness.
  This lies in the Noble Eightfold Path.

The Buddha taught that there is a cure for all the suffering people experience. The cure lies in following the Noble Eightfold Path (*see pages 18–19*). This is sometimes referred to as the middle way, because the Buddha chose a path between hardship and luxury.

The Dhamma: Noble Eightfold Path

The Buddha taught the Noble Eightfold Path, or middle way, to help people overcome the suffering he explained in the Four Noble Truths. The Path requires Buddhists to develop three essential characteristics: wisdom, ethics (doing the right thing), and mental effort.

WISDOM

In order to gain wisdom, a Buddhist has to master Right Understanding and Right Thought or Emotion.

Right Understanding: to see life as it is explained in the Four Noble Truths.
This comes first, as a person will not get anywhere unless he or she sees life as it really is.

Right Thought or Emotion: to be unselfish and show compassion to others.
This means that to become enlightened a person must be dedicated to following the *Dhamma*.

READING THE SCRIPTURES
People read the Buddha's teachings to help them cultivate the wisdom, ethics, and mental effort of the Noble Eightfold Path.

ETHICS

Buddhists should learn to do the right thing in every area of life. This means gaining Right Speech, Right Action, and Right Livelihood.

Right Speech: to tell the truth and speak kindly and gently.
Sometimes the truth can hurt, so sensitive words are essential. It is very important not to cause harm through speech, such as by saying things about someone behind their back.

Right Action: to live by the Five Precepts (see page 14).
Actions are truly right only if they are guided by good intentions. So if a person is kind, it must be purely for the benefit of others, and not because he or she wants something in return. Buddhists can guide their intentions and actions by developing compassion.

Right Livelihood: to work in harmony with the Dhamma.
The job a Buddhist does should not take advantage of people or the planet. It must not involve unfairness and should be helpful to others. Some Buddhists in the West, for example, work for educational trusts, Buddhist publishers, or health food stores.

MENTAL EFFORT

A healthy mind is as important as a healthy body, and Buddhists believe that discipline of the mind through Right Effort, Right Mindfulness, and Right Concentration is essential for a happy and purposeful life.

Right Effort: to be aware of inner feelings.
It also means being able to change negative moods and thoughts—when feeling sad, unfriendly, or angry—into positive ones such as being happy, friendly, and calm.

Right Mindfulness: to concentrate on and enjoy the actual living moment, at this exact time.
Right Mindfulness is how someone cultivates Right Effort. People often worry about the future, regret things from the past, and rush to get things done. This may get worse as a person grows older. Buddhists believe it makes people suffer. Right Mindfulness means changing all this and making the most of each moment.

Right Concentration (Right Meditation): to practice meditation.
All Buddhists practice meditation to help them cultivate Right Effort, Right Mindfulness, and lead what they call a more skillful life. Meditation can take many forms, but its goal is always to train the mind to become calm and positive.

THE NOBLE EIGHTFOLD PATH			
CHARACTERISTICS:	WISDOM	ETHICS	MENTAL EFFORT
PATHS:	Right Understanding	Right Speech	Right Effort
	Right Thought or Emotion	Right Action	Right Mindfulness
		Right Livelihood	Right Concentration

THE EIGHT-SPOKED WHEEL

The Buddha taught that people should practice all eight parts of the Noble Eightfold Path at the same time. That is why a major symbol for Buddhists is the eight-spoked wheel, or *dhammachakra* (wheel of the *Dhamma*). Each spoke plays an important part in supporting the wheel, which will lead the way to enlightenment.

THE EIGHT-SPOKED WHEEL
This wheel is the *dhammachakra*, which represents the Noble Eightfold Path to enlightenment.

Places of worship

Buddhists worship in two main types of buildings: monasteries and temples. All places of worship include a shrine room, containing an image of the Buddha, where worshipers can pay their respects and make offerings (*see pages 22–25*), just as they did when the Buddha was alive.

MONASTERIES

Monasteries, sometimes called *viharas*, are found in most towns and villages in Buddhist countries. They are places where the *Dhamma* is taught and monks and nuns live.

TEMPLES

Buddhist monks and nuns also live in temples. These take a variety of shapes and styles. Two typical types are pagodas—delicate, domed buildings found especially in China and Japan—and stupas. Stupas are mounds of stone built over what are believed to be relics of the Buddha. Buddhist temples are always designed to symbolize five elements of the universe: fire, air, water, earth (symbolized by the square base of the building), and wisdom (symbolized by the pinnacle at the top of the temple).

THE GOLDEN TEMPLE, JAPAN
Pagodas in China and Japan often look like this. They are viewed as symbols of happiness by the people who live nearby.

THE GOLDEN PAGODA, YANGON, MYANMAR
A pagoda is built in five sections. Each section represents one of five elements: earth, fire, water, wind, and wisdom.

THE BUDDHA'S IMAGE

All Buddhist places of worship contain a picture or statue of the Buddha. These can vary considerably according to where they are found. Part of the reason for the differences is that the teaching of the Buddha is considered much more important than his image—it is a teaching for all people in all places. In Bodh Gaya, where the Buddha became enlightened, there are several Buddhist temples dotted around the village. One is Japanese, another is Chinese, another is Thai—and in each one the image of the Buddha has characteristics that are typical of its country's own culture.

PLACES OF PILGRIMAGE

Buddhists go on pilgrimages to gain merit and blessings, which they hope will help them towards a better life when they are reborn. There are four main pilgrimage sites in and around India, all connected with the life of the Buddha.

LUMBINI GROVE

At Lumbini Grove, near Kepelavastu in Nepal, a stone pillar marks the Buddha's birthplace. It was put there by Emperor Ashoka (268–233 B.C.), who founded the first great Indian empire. He converted to Buddhism and devoted the rest of his life to spreading the *Dhamma*.

BODH GAYA

In Bodh Gaya, northern India, pilgrims visit the tree that is believed to be a descendant of the original Bodhi, or enlightenment, tree. This stands next to the Mahabodhi temple. The area also contains what is said to be the Buddha's footprint.

SARNATH

A few hundred miles away from Bodh Gaya lies the city of Varanasi. The deer park at Sarnath, just outside Varanasi, is where the Buddha preached his first sermon. The original deer park still exists, and a huge stupa built by Ashoka stands there. It is now a popular place of pilgrimage.

KUSINARA

At Kusinara, where the Buddha died (or reached *parinibbana*), there stands the Nibbana Temple and Stupa, another important site for devoted pilgrims.

Places of pilgrimage in other countries include: Sri Pada in Sri Lanka, where a footprint of the Buddha marks the spot where he came ashore; the Temple of the Sacred Tooth in Kandy, also in Sri Lanka; and the Golden Pagoda in Yangon, Myanmar (*left*), which contains a relic of the Buddha's hair.

THE MAHABODHI TEMPLE, INDIA

This temple is situated in Bodh Gaya in northern India, the place where the Buddha reached enlightenment.

A STUPA

This stupa marks the place where the Buddha preached his first sermon in the deer park in Sarnath.

Buddhist worship

STATUE OF THE BUDDHA
The Buddha image, or *rupa*, is the main focus for Buddhist worship. It reminds all Buddhists that they can become enlightened.

The focus of Buddhist worship is not God, but the Buddha. The word usually used to describe this worship is *puja*. *Puja* helps Buddhists to develop positive attitudes such as determination and joy, which make practicing the *Dhamma* easier.

THE SHRINE

Buddhists worship and make offerings to a shrine in order to thank the Buddha for giving them the *Dhamma*. The offerings also remind Buddhists that they too can reach enlightenment.

THE BUDDHA RUPA

The central focus of a Buddhist shrine, and of Buddhist worship, is the Buddha image, or *rupa*. It has various symbolic parts which help to inspire the worshiper.

The bulge on top of the *rupa's* head, called the *ushnisha*, symbolizes wisdom and enlightenment. The *rupa's* long ear lobes remind followers that the Buddha once wore the earrings of an Indian prince who gave up worldly power. The spot in the center of his forehead stands for the "third eye," called the "*Dhamma* eye." This traditional Indian symbol can also be seen on images of Hindu gods such as Shiva, reminding us that Buddhism developed from Hinduism, the religion that the Buddha was born into.

The *rupa* shows the Buddha wearing a plain robe, which represents his simple life. His face always shows great calm and compassion, and the figure usually sits in the cross-legged lotus position—a pose which people who meditate often use to help them sit still for long periods of time. The *rupa* may sit on a lotus flower, which is a symbol of enlightenment.

A very important part of the *rupa* is the position of the hands. They form a *mudra* (symbolic gesture). There are many different *mudras* and they all symbolize different things. The most common are the *mudras* for fearlessness, teaching, and meditation.

THE FEARLESSNESS MUDRA

When the hand is held in front of the chest with the palm turned outward it represents fearlessness (*see right*). The Buddha is reassuring people not be afraid.

FEARLESSNESS MUDRA
This *rupa* is from Myanmar. The fearlessness mudra symbolizes protection and peace.

THE TEACHING MUDRA

In the teaching *mudra* the hand is raised with the tips of the forefinger and thumb touching each other (*see far right*). This represents the turning of the wheel of the *Dhamma*.

THE MEDITATION MUDRA

Hands resting together in the lap with the palms upwards and the thumbs touching symbolize meditation (*see below*). The thumbs touch to form a nerve channel, which helps the mind towards enlightenment.

TEACHING MUDRA
This *rupa* is from Sri Lanka. It clearly shows the *Dhamma* eye and long ear lobes that are characteristic of many *rupas*.

In Mahayana shrines there may also be other images showing *bodhisattvas*, in particular Avalokiteshvara and Tara, different forms of the *bodhisattva* of compassion, and Manjushri, the *bodhisattva* of wisdom.

MEDITATION MUDRA
This rupa in Sri Lanka has been carved from solid rock.

OFFERINGS MADE TO THE SHRINE

The offerings that Buddhists make to the shrine include candles, flowers, and incense. These have important symbolic meanings.

The light of a candle: this reminds Buddhists of the Buddha's wisdom, which they believe lit up people's minds.

The flowers: these stand for impermanence and change. Flowers are beautiful things, but after a short while they wither and die.

The incense: this represents caring feelings, which lead to good actions. Just as the scent of incense spreads throughout a building, so good actions can influence others and spread around the world.

Most shrines also have seven water-filled offering bowls that symbolize the seven things traditionally offered in India to an honored guest. These are water for washing, water to drink, flowers to garland the visitor, incense, light, perfume, and food. Buddhists offer these to the Buddha as the honored guest.

A Buddhist usually makes an offering to the *rupa* when he or she enters the shrine room. This often involves lighting incense sticks and bowing down low in front of the image. Sometimes Buddhists chant to remind themselves about the meaning of making offerings to the *rupa*.

OFFERINGS

Top: Buddhists light candles to represent enlightenment, and offer incense (*above*) to the shrine to represent caring feelings.

MEDITATION

Opposite: Meditation helps Buddhists on their journey to enlightenment.

MEDITATION

Buddhists meditate because it helps them to achieve a calm, positive state of mind and come closer to enlightenment. There are two basic types of meditation—*samatha*, which means calm, and *vipassana*, which means insight. To be a skillful Buddhist, a person needs to practice both types.

Samatha meditation helps Buddhists to develop mindfulness. When someone begins this type of meditation, he or she focuses all concentration on his or her breathing. This allows the person to ignore thoughts in his or her head. Eventually, the person feels calm and able to concentrate more deeply.

Vipassana meditation is about watching and understanding how thoughts arise in the mind. It is about training the mind and realizing that a person's thoughts influence the way he or she experiences things. For example, if someone is in a bad mood, it affects the way he or she treats others. *Vipassana* meditation tries to show that these moods are not the "real" person because they do not last. Becoming skilled at *Vipassana* means that a Buddhist will be more likely to treat people with loving kindness (*metta*) and compassion (*karuna*).

Families and life rituals

A BUDDHIST WEDDING
The celebration of a marriage is important for Buddhists.

The only religious life-cycle ceremonies that Buddhists perform are ordinations and funerals. They do not have particular religious ceremonies for birth or marriage, though these are considered important, and families may ask for blessings at that time from the monks and nuns.

MARRIAGE AND FAMILY LIFE

Only about five percent of Buddhists are ordained monks or nuns. The rest are lay Buddhists, and for them family life is very important. A central idea in Buddhism is "spiritual friendship." This refers to all relationships in life, but especially between husband and wife.

Although there is no religious ritual for joining husband and wife, marriage is still celebrated. In Theravada countries, a cotton thread may be placed around the statue of the Buddha and linked to everyone present.

The thread is then cut and tied around the wrists of the groom and bride. They wear these "bracelets" until they fall off. Monks do not perform the ceremonies, but they may bless the marriage in a separate service.

The *Sutta Pitaka* (*see pages 12–13*) contains advice from the Buddha on how to have a successful and happy married life. Husbands should provide for their wives and be polite, respectful, and faithful to them. In return, wives should be faithful, practical, and hospitable to relatives. There are also rules for parents and children. Children should support their parents in a number of ways, and parents should guide, educate, and protect their children.

BIRTH AND UPBRINGING

Traditionally, a Buddhist mother will receive a blessing from the temple monks before she gives birth. After the birth, the baby will be taken to the temple to be blessed by a monk or nun and sprinkled with holy water.

Parents may ask for a special Buddhist name for the child. In countries such as Myanmar and Thailand, young boys may become ordained as monks for a short period of time as part of their spiritual education.

BLESSING CHILDREN
Babies and young children are blessed by monks to show how special they are.

THE HOME SHRINE

Most Buddhist families have their own shrine at home, complete with a statue of the Buddha. Here they provide offerings and perform *puja* (worship) daily, but especially on full moon or festival days. Some families attend local temples on special days and take part in *dana* (an act of generosity in which they give food to the monks and nuns).

DEATH

Death is very significant for Buddhists because it is connected with rebirth. It is most important that they have a "good" death. This means being peaceful and thinking correctly about what death means. Buddhists should see and accept dying as part of the impermanence of life. When someone is dying, a monk or nun may be asked to chant scriptures to remind the person of the Buddha's teaching. This will help cultivate a calm mind.

Buddhists are usually cremated when they die, but burial does sometimes take place. Funerals are conducted by monks. They highlight the positive qualities of the dead person. Sometimes people who are present at the service meditate to ask forgiveness from the dead person for any wrongs they may have done to them. Likewise, they may be asked to forgive the dead person for any wrongs he or she has carried out. All this will help the dead person to have a better life next time.

A SHRINE AT HOME
Most Buddhists have a home shrine so they can constantly remember the Buddha's gift of the *Dhamma*.

27

Buddhist festivals are based on the lunar calendars of particular countries. These calendars depend on the shape and position of the moon in the sky, so the festival dates vary accordingly. The meanings of festivals also vary according to the culture of the Buddhist group concerned.

Most Buddhist festivals include a time when lay people come to the temple, or *vihara,* and join in with the monks' activities. They bring offerings and food for the monks. They chant scriptures, listen to teachings, and meditate. Festivals offer Buddhists a chance to renew their commitment to the Five Precepts (*see page 14–15*) and other teachings. Some lay members take on extra precepts such as fasting for a short time.

LIGHTING LAMPS FOR WESAK

Wesak is the most important festival for Buddhists, when they remember the birth, enlightenment, and death of the Buddha.

HANAMATSURI

Hanamatsuri celebrates the Buddha's birth.

WESAK

The most important Theravada Buddhist festival is *Wesak* (also known as *Vaisakha Puja).* It is celebrated in such countries as Sri Lanka and Thailand and takes place on the day of the full moon in May. It commemorates the Buddha's birth, enlightenment, and *parinibbana.* Mahayana Buddhists also celebrate these events in a separate festival. They have one day for each stage, with the enlightenment on Bodhi Day in December. The Friends of the Western Buddhist Order in the West celebrate Buddha Day. *Wesak* often involves lighting candles to symbolize the way the Buddha's teachings light up the world.

HANAMATSURI

Hanamatsuri is a Japanese Mahayana Buddhist festival and takes place in the West in April. It is a flower festival celebrating the Buddha's birth in the garden at Lumbini. A model of the infant Buddha is bathed and set in a floral shrine. The word *hana* is Japanese for "flower," and *matsuri* means "festival."

KATHINA DAY

Kathina Day takes place at the end of the rainy season in southern Asian countries, such as Sri Lanka. During this time, the rains made it difficult for the Buddha and his monks to travel and teach. In the West, *Kathina* is celebrated in October. It is a joyful ceremony in which lay members offer new robes to the monks.

PARINIBBANA

This is a Mahayana festival which, in the West, is celebrated in February. It marks the death of the Buddha. He is said to have died because he ate some poisonous mushrooms. Buddhists believe that he passed away in a state of meditation, reclining on his side with his head in his hand. This can be seen in pictures and statues of the Buddha.

POSON DAY

This Sri Lankan festival is held on the day of the full moon in June. It celebrates the coming of Buddhism to Sri Lanka in 246 B.C., when Mahinda, Emperor Ashoka's son, converted King Tissa to Buddhism. In Sri Lanka, *Poson* is celebrated with a colorful parade. Huge floats carry images telling the story of Mahinda and the king. For Sri Lankan Buddhists in the West, there is a day-long program of chanting, meditation, and talks about Mahinda in the *vihara*.

ASALA DAY

This festival takes place on the day of the full moon in July, and celebrates the time when the Buddha preached his first sermon in the deer park at Sarnath. At *Asala*, the whole of the Buddha's sermon is chanted to mark the start of his teaching. In Kandy in Sri Lanka, there are spectacular parades involving more than 100 beautifully decorated elephants, accompanied by dancers, drummers, and acrobats.

There are a great many more Buddhist festivals celebrated in countries such as Tibet and China. Many of these mark the same events in the Buddha's life, but some are unique to each country.

ASALA DAY
Elephant parades in Kandy, Sri Lanka, celebrate the Buddha's first sermon at Sarnath.

29

Key questions and answers

WHAT IS BUDDHISM? Buddhism is the main religion in such countries as Sri Lanka, Bhutan, Myanmar, Thailand, Cambodia, and Vietnam. Followers of Buddhism are called Buddhists. The Buddhist community is called the *Sangha* (*see pages 10–11*).

HOW MANY BUDDHISTS ARE THERE? Approximately 328 million.

WHAT FORMS OF BUDDHISM ARE THERE? Mahayana (Tibetan, Zen, and Pure Land Buddhism) and Theravada (*see pages 4–5*).

WHAT DO BUDDHISTS BELIEVE? Buddhists do not believe in God; instead they follow the teachings of the Buddha (*see pages 6–7*). Buddhists aim to become enlightened like the Buddha by snuffing out the three poisons to reach *nibbana* (*see pages 8–9*). Buddhists make a commitment to the Three Jewels (*see page 10*).

WHAT ARE THE BUDDHA'S TEACHINGS CALLED? Buddha taught the *Dhamma*: the Four Noble Truths (*see pages 16–17*) and the Noble Eightfold Path or "middle way" (*see pages 18–19*).

WHAT ARE THE BUDDHIST SCRIPTURES CALLED? The different types of scriptures include the "three baskets" (the *Vinaya Pitaka, Sutta Pitaka,* and *Abhidamma Pitaka*), the Lotus *Sutta,* and the Heart and Diamond *Sutta* (*see pages 12–13*).

WHAT ARE THE BUDDHIST RULES FOR LIVING? The Five Precepts underpin all of Buddhist life. In addition, monks and nuns follow the *vinaya* (rules of monastic life). They include a total of 227 precepts (*see pages 14–15*).

WHERE DO BUDDHISTS WORSHIP? Buddhists worship in temples and monasteries (*see page 20*). All these places contain a picture or *rupa* of the Buddha (*see pages 22–23*). Many Buddhists have a shrine at home (*see page 27*).

WHAT ARE THE MAIN BUDDHIST FESTIVALS? *Wesak, Hanamatsuri, Kathina* Day, *Paranibbana, Poson* Day, and *Asala* Day (*see pages 28–29*).

Glossary

ANNICA The impermanence of all things, according to Buddhist teaching.

ARAHAT According to Theravada Buddhism, a person who has reached the end of the Noble Eightfold Path and realized the truth about life and human suffering.

BODHISATTVA A person who is on the way to being enlightened, but postpones enlightenment to help others. Also, an enlightened person who returns to the world to help others toward enlightenment.

BODHI TREE The tree under which the Buddha became enlightened. *Bodhi* is an Indian term that means enlightenment.

DALAI LAMA The spiritual leader of Tibetan Buddhists and the exiled leader of Tibet.

DANA Generosity or giving.

DHAMMA Universal law or eternal truth. For Buddhists, it is the teachings of the Buddha, which they believe did not originate with Siddhattha. The historical Buddha "uncovered" the teachings, which exist independent of him and had remained hidden for years.

DUKKHA Suffering, unsatisfactoriness. According to Buddhism, the basic disease of human nature from which people need to be liberated.

GAYA A town in northeast India. Nearby is Bodh Gaya, which marks the place where the Buddha became enlightened. It is now a place of pilgrimage for Buddhists.

HANAMATSURI A flower festival celebrated in April by Japanese Mahayana Buddhists. This remembers the Buddha's birth in the garden at Lumbini. A model of the infant Buddha is often bathed and set in a floral shrine.

KAMMA Action that has causes and effects, and influences a person's future life.

KARUNA Compassion.

KATHINA DAY A festival celebrated in October by Theravada Buddhists, when the lay members offer new robes to the monks.

LOTUS FLOWER The flower of a water-lily, the traditional Indian symbol of enlightenment.

MAHAYANA BUDDHISM A form of Buddhism that stresses compassion in the form of a *bodhisattva*.

MEDITATION A practice that calms the mind and body, and helps a person achieve enlightenment.

METTA Loving kindness.

NIBBANA A snuffing out of the three poisons—greed, hatred, and ignorance—leading to a state of bliss.

PAGODA A Buddhist temple in five sections, symbolizing the five elements of the universe.

PALI CANON The earliest and most complete form of Buddhist scriptures.

PARINIBBANA The final state of bliss into which the Buddha entered at his death.

RUPA An image of the Buddha.

SANGHA The Buddhist community. One of the three refuges or three jewels, the other two being the Buddha and the *Dhamma*.

SARNATH The town, about 5 miles (4 km) outside the holy city of Varanasi in India, where the Buddha preached his first sermon, in a deer park.

SIDDHATTHA GOTAMA The name of the historical Buddha.

STUPA A religious building that contains a relic (part of a holy person's body or belongings) of the Buddha.

TANHA Desire or craving. The cause of suffering.

THERAVADA BUDDHISM The "way of the elders," the oldest form of Buddhism.

VINAYA The rules and discipline of monastic life.

WESAK Celebration of the birth, life, teachings, and death of the Buddha.

Index